OKLAHOMA POEMS

...

AND THEIR POETS

D1260280

MEZCALITA PRESS, LLC – Norman, OK

COVER DESIGN: Jen Rickard Blair

COVER ART: "Tall Cotton" by Rick Sinnett

MEZCALITA PRESS, LLC
Norman, Oklahoma

Also on MEZCALITA PRESS:

Karma Crisis: New & Selected Poems by Nathan Brown
Less Is More, More or Less by Nathan Brown

ii

OKLAHOMA
POEMS

...

AND THEIR POETS

O

Edited by

NATHAN BROWN

2013 – 2014
Poet Laureate of Oklahoma

TABLE OF CONTENTS

PLACES

ODDS & ENDS

ACKNOWLEDGEMENTS

—To the OKLAHOMA HUMANITIES COUNCIL.

—To Jen Rickard Blair for all the great work on graphic and cover design.

—To Rick Sinnett for the use of his beautiful piece "Tall Cotton."

—To WORLD LITERATURE TODAY for their support of this project.

—To my wife, and the best editor I know: Ashley Brown.

○

Oklahoma is the state that raised me. And though I may not have believed it when I was a teenager, it turns out to be a good parent. It keeps a close eye on you, in case you're about to do something stupid. But it comes to all your games and yells for you too.

As I approach 50, I can easily say that no matter where I travel, or where I may live, Oklahoma is, and will always be, home. I call it my home with a reverence, as well as with a deep love. And I know many other folks who call it their home with the same reverence—even a few good souls who claim it as home with a vengeance.

This book is a small taste of what I'm talking about.

~ Nathan Brown

OKLAHOMA POEMS

In Memory of Jim Chastain…

THE LAST SONG

~ Joy Harjo

how can you stand it
he said
the hot oklahoma summers
where you were born
this humid thick air
is choking me
and i want to go back
to new mexico

it is the only way
i know how to breathe
an ancient chant
that my mother knew
came out of a history
woven from wet tall grass
in her womb
and i know no other way
than to surround my voice
with the summer songs of crickets
in this moist south night air

oklahoma will be the last song
i'll ever sing

PEOPLE

When the Okies left Oklahoma and moved to California, they raised the average intelligence level in both states.

~ Will Rogers

RED MOON POWWOW
(Cheyenne Nation, Hammon, Oklahoma, 2006)

~ Dorothy Alexander

Tribal drums tremble the night air.
Dog Soldiers stomp a fancy dance,
turkey feathers bob and weave,
Converse All Stars and Nike Hi-Tops
slap rhythm on the packed earth.

The whole Cheyenne Nation sits on folding
chairs, eating Frito chili pies and fry bread.
Spotted Bird's widow, Christine Star,
daughter to Old Man Fingernail and Martha
Swallow, waits for the give-away to begin,
rechecking her list of those she will honor,

giving them baskets stuffed with bags
of Yukon's Best corn meal and flour,
Domino sugar, made-in-China junk
from Wal-Mart. Plus one fine Pendleton
blanket and a carton of unfiltered Camels
for the Keeper of the Sacred Arrows.

Imogene Old Crow paces back and forth,
her shadow dancing in firelight, carrying on
a cell phone conversation, Blue-Tooth loop
clipped to her crow black hair. She listens
to the sacred drums with one ear,
the profane world with the other one.

YELLOW COTTONWOODS

~ Ken Hada

There's heartache in these lines
cracking through once-hard ground
crumbling to course dust.

Sadness drifts here
beneath these yellow Cottonwoods
where old men sit
in distorted circles – a parlor
for the ornery and rejected –
where a can of beer
accompanies a well-worn story
told with fading bravado
fear swallowed in quick gulps.

These grains of river sand
dry in wind, sifting
through time, piled around toes
of shuffling boots, legs
dangling off a tailgate or
sitting awry in a chair
whose fabric is stretched
past the point of brittle.

An Evening in Kingfisher

~ George Economou

"Entering Kingfisher, Oklahoma"
the road sign reads
"The Buckle on the Wheat Belt."
We drive to the Elks Club
where we join three hundred men
with big buckles on their belts
to boost the Sooners & our university
in what is traditionally OSU Aggie territory
drinking & mixing with them, eating "fries"
also known as prairie or mountain oysters
scooped up barehanded
as you hold your beer or bourbon in the other
followed by steaks, ranch style baked beans
homemade cracked wheat bread & more beer
salad fixings with no dressing whatever
strong coffee & no fooling around with dessert.
After the obligatory welcome speeches
the winningest active coach in college football
runs the play he will call this spring
a hundred times throughout the state
and then fields questions:
—"Barry (pronounced Berra), how's the Texas
    game gone turn out this year?"
—"One thing I kin tell you 'bout the Texas
    game fer sure—it's gone be one tough
sumabitch!"
—"Barry, could yuh use a sixty-six year old guard?"
—"Give that man another drink."
Somebody does as coach Switzer
closes this appearance with a herpes joke
and a hopeful, if not overconfident

prediction about the coming season.
The macho party & male ritual complete
(except for those with expectations
based on their consumption of fries)
we move for the doors or bartenders
and I am almost out into the night air
when the sixty-six year old guard pulls
out of the line at the bar & squints
at my crimson-bordered OU name tag
offering his hand to mine which he begins to squeeze
and asks me where I'm from.
—"The university."
—"Well, I kin see that. I mean with a name
   like that where are yuh *from?*"
Looking back at his tag
which reads "'Huck' Rice"
and understanding what he's getting at,
—"Just moved here from New York,
   but I was born in Montana."
He squeezes harder,
—"But that's not an American name."
—"Sure it is, from Greece. (And making a good
guess)
   When did your people come over here from
Germany, Huck?"
Easing up on the squeeze,
—"Oh hell, we bin here forever."
—"You mean you're Native American?"
—"No, no Indian. What d'yuh do at OU?"
—"I teach English."
—With a name like that, yuh teach English?"
—"I run the whole show in English, Huck.
   I'm chairman of the department, brought in

10

from New York."
The handshake ends in a tie
and I am grateful for the summers
spent opening oysters in Wellfleet.
—"Well, George, how d'yuh like workin'
    here among all these Americans?"
—"I told you, Huck, I was *born* here."
—"I like yuh, George, I'd like to talk
    to yuh 'bout your beliefs."
Remembering Roy Rogers' characterization
of Reagan when he was nominated in 1980,
—"Why, I'm 'a fine Christian gentleman,'
    just like you. Only my kind is the oldest,
    Huck. Greek, you know, right back to the
    language of the New Testament (making another
    good guess) while you Lutherans are pretty
recent."
Shaking his head,
—"Greek, and yuh teach English
    and don't even have an accent."
—"No, no accent, Huck, perfect English.
    You've got the accent. But give me a
    chance and I'll be back here next year
    sounding just like you."
—"I'd like that, I like yuh, George."
—"So long, Huck, see you next year."
Leaving Kingfisher, I try not to hear
the obvious literary echoes
and focus rather on the odd sincerity
of my dialogue with Huck,
and definitely name him
to my first team offensive line.

FLINN, ON THE BUS

~ Naomi Shihab Nye

Three hours after the buildings fell,
he took a seat beside me.
Fresh out of prison, after 24 months,
You're my first hello!
Going home to Mom,
a life he would make better this time,
how many times
he'd been swept along before,
to things he should never have...
drink and dope,
but now he'd take responsibility.
Lawyers had done him wrong
and women too. He thought
about revenge, now he was out.
But I'm in charge. I'll think
before I act. I don't ever
want to go there again.
Two wrongs don't make a right.
Somehow, in his mouth, that day,
it sounded new.
The light came through the window
on a gentle-eyed man in a
"Focus on the Game" T-shirt,
who had given up
assault with deadly weapons,
no more, no good!
A man who had not seen TV in weeks,
secluding in his cell so colleagues
wouldn't trip him up,
extend his stay.
Who had not heard the news.

We rolled through green Oklahoma,
the bus windows made all the trees look bent.
A trick of refraction –
Flinn looked at his free hands
more than the fields,
turned them over in his lap,
no snap judgments, no quick angers,
I'll stand back, look at what happens,
think calmly what my next step should be.
It was not hard to nod,
to wish him well. But could I tell
what had happened in the world
on his long-awaited day,
what twists of rage greater
than we could ever guess
had savaged skylines, thousands of lives?
I could not. He'd find out
soon enough. Flinn, take it easy.
Peace is rough.

Sept. 11, 2001

MEDITATION ON A THEME OF SAM BAKER

~ Steven Schroeder

That all
the water is
sparkling seems

undeniable
in this light.
Sudden rain

takes the edge
off Oklahoma
heat at sunset.

There is music
in the rain, in
the red

horizon, in
the red dirt, in
the hands, in

the voices, in
this body of friends,
remembering.

Drink it all in
you must be present to win.

PICTURES OF PIONEER WOMEN

~ Abigail Keegan

You can see from their faces,
life offered little to smile about.
Wet or dry, rutted roads, if they
existed, wrenched and yanked axles.
Settlements ramshackle as card stacks
set up for gambling fell together.

And when there were no streets
or houses, only sod dwellings,
cows came morning and afternoon,
afternoon and morning from fields
and the far ends of a brutal sun,
udders caked in red dust or red mud.

Sleeves and skirts, wrists to ankles,
shoulders broadened by swinging an axe,
backs humped like twisted wind-blown
trees from donkeying strapping loads.

A stalwart few, rare as prairie summer rain,
were photographed next to bearded husbands
and a dozen children. Look, they peer fiercely
forward, as we look carefully back.

Tulsa Pool Player

~ James Navé

He played pool, that boy from Tulsa; his name was
Jack and he could scatter those pool balls like
rainbows over a green sky. He was dusty; his hands
were quick; and his deep eyes won hearts. "Never
more than two light bulbs above my table," Jack
would say, "I don't like to squint while I win." Fifty
dollars and enough stamina to play all night would
get you into one of Jack's games.

All the boys smoked and leaned forward as they
watched the pool balls orbit straight into the hungry
corners. Jack's mouth was always open just a little
bit, and when he smiled, you could hear the money
rustling in his pockets. Even the rack boys stood still
on the afternoon Jack's cue ball nicked a yellow nine
and spun into the corner. When the ball dropped,
Jack stood quiet for a second, puffed his Lucky, and
said, "Boys, drinks are on me."

The day after Jack left town, the boys started
claiming their cue balls were running just a little
straighter. On Christmas Eve, word came back that a
black-haired West Texas girl from the Apache
Mountains had spun past Jack on the break and left
him two thousand down by dawn. They said it didn't
bother Jack a bit. He just leaned his cue stick against
the wall, smiled, and bought her cup of coffee. When
this story bounced around the pool hall, the boys
tipped their glasses back, laughed out loud, and left
every cue stick standing at attention.

CHOCTAW BINGO

~ James McMurtry
(excerpt from the song)

Uncle Slayton's
got his Texan pride
back in the thickets
with his Asian bride.

He's got an Airstream trailer
and a Holstein cow.
He still makes whiskey
'cause he still knows how.

He plays that Choctaw bingo
every Friday night. You know,
he had to leave Texas,
but he won't say why.

He owns a quarter section
up by Lake Eufala.
Caught a great big ol' blue cat
on a driftin' jug line.

Sells his hardwood timber
to the chippin' mill.
Cooks that crystal meth
because the shine don't sell.

He cooks that crystal meth
because the shine don't sell.
You know he likes that money,
he don't mind the smell.

THANKSGIVING

~ Julia McConnell

We'd say *Blesses*
Owl Lord
No, that's my Okie.
Try again.

Blesses Our Lord
And these thine gifts...
Your bounty Christ...
You are thinking
too hard.
Try again.

Bless us, Oh Lord
for these thine gifts
which we are about to receive...
Just Google it.

This prayer I never
thought I would forget.

I wriggled in my chair
when asked to recite
it at dinner.
Felt churning in my stomach
as an altar girl ringing
the bells at consecration.

Now I am trying
to remember
how to say grace.

Oklahoma Ghazal

~ Daniel Simon

Traversed by migrants obsessed with home
haunted by ghosts dispossessed from home

aboriginals, arrivistes, dirt poor, nouveau riche
inundated with longing for a mythical home

suspicious of quitclaims and shell games
jaded by outsiders who might swindle their homes

clinging to the land after too many sky-betrayals
every flat slab a promise of everlasting home

each act of faith in raising and redemption, Daniel
a belief that we don't live in, but inhabit, our home

My Grandfather and His Eggs

~ Lauren Camp

My Papa raised the flattened sun on a Tulsa sky
each weekday morning. Tall and hollow,

he was suspended in a life sunny side up.
Nine to 5, he candled eggs, sorted them by color

then headed home to boiled eggs. Papa played piano.
He carried his lungs in a shirt pocket, his humor

in a highball glass. Sometimes Papa painted portraits;
his life was drawn in charcoal.

Papa steeped his eggs in oleo. Papa fried his fears.
On weekends, Papa walked nine holes of golf

then sank into his armchair. Papa lit a cigarette.
Papa by TV, Papa with his glasses.

My mom was fragile when he died.
We watched her eyes go runny,

how she slid into the pan
of what was missing.

I tell you grief can lay eggs anywhere.
Pale and delicate, Mom dreamt her daddy

in the bowl of heaven.
She saw Papa in her photos, heard Papa

in her whispers. Papa drinking gin,
Papa over easy. Now Mom has moved

through that same membrane, and without her,
life in our house keeps breaking open.

LEARNING TO SPEAK CHOCTAW

~ Ron Wallace

He rose like smoke from high grass
and weeds that had taken the alley
east of the Katy tracks
and shuffled across the gravel road
     black hair, black eyes,
a hundred creases in a dark brown face.

A brown hand lifted
as he saw my father bent under the hood
of his red Chevy.

"Halito, Leonard Wallace, chim achukma?"

His long sleeves pulled his hands inside
khaki pockets.

Dad's head remained in the motor
     "Hello, Earl,
I'm fine. Need a ride to town?"

"Jus' walkin', Captain.
Headed for Red's, get me a hamburger
     if you spot me a quarter
'til I mow some lawns."

I stopped bouncing the rubber ball
off the shed,
eyed the worn brogans on his feet,
and glanced at Dad still buried in his Chevy.

He looked at me and my beat up ball glove.

"Halito, Little Wallace,
you the next, Allie Reynolds?"
I shrugged
        he grinned.
"Keep throwing that ball; you be
another Super Chief."

Dad pulled a handful of coins
from his pockets
        selected a silver quarter
and flipped it to the old Choctaw.

"Yokoke, my policeman friend.
I owe you four quarters now; I know.
        I go eat now."

He moved like tall grass in an easy wind
up the gravel road
to the railroad track and out of sight
        my eyes following in his wake.

"War and wine,
goddamned war and wine,"
        Dad melted back
into the Chevy's engine;
"Throw the ball, Son,
        just keep throwin' the ball."

A RED BARN FOR THE JOADS

~ Norbert Krapf

We could allow the ghostly Okies
wandering in the rain to discover
this dry barn. Their jalopy truck
sputtered and died on the road again.

The Joads, who lost their farm
to the banks and Grandpa
and Grandma to the road, could
stagger in by the side door.

If they happen to find
a young boy whose emaciated
father lies dying on the floor,
Ma, who rises to every occasion,
could take charge and speak fiery
words again. Pa could stand and stare
while firebrand brother Tom is off
fighting for a scrap of dignity.

Rose of Sharon, who just lost
her first baby, could give
the old man her breast, under
a blanket. The animals would
all understand, but some people
might not. Worse things happened
in our families during the Depression.
Lots worse could happen in red
barns all over southern Indiana.

PLACES

Okemah was one of the singiest, square dancingest, drinkingest, yellingest, preachingest, walkingest, talkingest, laughingest, cryingest, shootingest, fist fightingest, bleedingest, gamblingest, gun, club and razor carryingest of our ranch towns and farm towns, because it blossomed out into one of our first Oil Boom Towns.

~ WOODY GUTHRIE

DEEP FORK

~ Ben Myers

This flat river gives red back to the sky
above it, both carrying dust and flakes

of clipped grass. I walk with a slight
limp into the middle of my life,

watch turtles raise
their heads in dead water,

in my pocket two crumpled rejection
notes from magazines on the coast.

A tree frog near my ear
begins its whine,

and I plan to cease my argument
with God about my little life.

I've been blessed with two
plots near the edge of town

and the opportunity to live
on the face of the southern plains.

I'm going to start wearing overalls
and riding an old tractor down Main.

I'll spend my days with these two
crows, see what it is they know.

Oklahoma City

~ Stephen Dunn

The accused chose to plead innocent
because he was guilty. We allowed such a thing;
it was one of our greatnesses, nutty, protective.
On the car radio a survivor's ordeal, her leg
amputated without anesthesia while trapped

under a steel girder. Simply, no big words—
that's how people tell their horror stories.
I was elsewhere, on my way to a party.
On arrival, everyone was sure to be carrying
a piece of the awful world with him.

Not one of us wouldn't be smiling.
There'd be drinks, irony, hidden animosities.
Something large would be missing.
But most of us would understand
something large always would be missing.

Oklahoma City was America reduced
to McVeigh's half-thought-out thoughts.
Did he know anything about suffering?
It's the naïve among us who are guilty
of wondering if we're moral agents or madmen

or merely, as one scientist said,
a fortuitous collocation of atoms.
Some mysteries can be solved by ampersands.
*And*s not *or*s; that was my latest answer.
At the party two women were talking

about how strange it is that they still like men.
They were young and unavailable, and their
    lovely faces
evoked a world not wholly incongruent
with the world I know. I had no illusions,
    not even hopes,
that their beauty had anything to do with goodness.

ON THE PLAINS

~ Larry D. Thomas

As Kansas
rises
in their kitchens,

readying
for browning
in their ovens,

and Nebraska,
with billions
of yellow ears

muffled
in shucks
of green,

listens
to their every
word,

Oklahoma
lies back
on prairie grass,

locks its hands
behind its head,
and muses

a sky bluer
than the blues
of Memphis.

VICI, OKLAHOMA

~ Diane Glancy

All afternoon you think how there's something
stronger than you,
the sky pale as jeans turned inside out.

Wind wrestles the house,
strong arms trees,
jumping electrical wires above the yard.

Once the day floated easy
as leeches in a jar of water from the horse tank.
The boy held them on his desk all day,
light through the jar
clear & steady as window glass.

Here on the plains, farmers wave when you pass
as though you had forgotten something,
as though you should turn back
before you step silently through the air
disappearing into light.

DRIVEWAY

~ Ron Padgett

Again I slid up over the horizon
and the lights of Tulsa spread flat out before me.
"Ah, there you are," I said,
"like a porch light left on
for almost thirty years."
                                "Don't get carried away,
Ron. Yes, the lights are on for you and anyone
else who wants to rush toward me in a stream of light,"
the awakened city said, "but I knew
it was you. Who else would talk to me like this?"
I said, "There always was this special thing between us,
no?"
        "Between you and me,
not between me and you. You're like all the rest,
you think you're the only one to come along, that
I was made for you."
                        "I know, Tulsa, but
remember, I was an only child."
                                "I know, Ron, but
you're not a child now, so why act like one?
Why don't you settle back and take a deep, long look
at things the way they are? Why not just let go
of your love-hate thing with me? Do you really need
this longing and regret and so much useless anger?"
"But what'll I have of the me who was a little boy?"
"Whatever you already have, no more, no less,"
the voice said evenly.
                        Suddenly I cried
into the dark, "Where's your mouth?"
"You don't know? It's all around you—"

I was pulling
into the driveway where I used to live
          "—it's your skin"
and opened my eyes and was
here, in New York, typing these lines.

WILL ROGERS TURNPIKE

~ Quraysh Ali Lansana

these roads my veins dry red
clay body sun smoke wafts heat
tired of itself wheezing semi-trailers
alfalfa between cheek and gum

cicada guitar twang ditties tink
powerline towers alien horizon
march shoulders hawk respite
in absence of elm and birch

dust devils square dance prairie
as christian clouds loft fervor
sun to our right only sky blue
this land our road hum and scent

something dead every quarter mile
what are you, mexican? the kind cracker
asks at truck stop amazed to learn
of duet between nelly and tim mcgraw

patience is the i-35 junction abrupt urban
merger   night a blindfold
headlights on city
licks chops and growls

THE ETYMOLOGY OF HONKY TONK

~ Jeanetta Calhoun Mish

Its dancing seeds arrived in Oklahoma Territory
along with those of red wheat and tumbleweed
hidden in the pockets of Russian German
  immigrants.
It was cultivated with a fiddle bow grasped
in the calloused hand of a Scots Irish farmer
and given the blues by freedmen
singing in black township road houses.
Its rhythm was established by a defiant Indian drum
echoing down a river valley in the spring.
Someone's little brother gave it words and
simple chords strummed on a mail-order guitar;
at the age of thirty it got some swing and
learned syncopatin' from a count and a duke.
Its lonesome cry slid in from Hawaii
twelve strings and two pedals on a hurricane wind.
Just yesterday it was crooning to a blue moon
and flirting with a saxophone player.

It is a sound and a song and a sanctuary;
it is a place and a plea and a prayer
and it calls you out to sit in with the band
because it knows you remember the tune.

The first known documented, print usage of the term
"honk-a-tonk" is found in *The Daily Ardmorite*
(Oklahoma), February 26, 1894.

CORDELL

~ George Bilgere

I drove the tiny, grasshopper green
motorcycle to the town's edge
and, for the first time,
bought gas, counting out dimes
and quarters to an old guy in a ball cap.

For the first time
I pondered the venous skin
of a map and charted a route from Burns Flat
to Cordell, a little town
on the Oklahoma plains. The day
was sparkling and unrehearsed, the air
cool in the morning, and for the first time
I went out on the public roads alone,
despite having no license, the world
for the first time passing in a rush
at the tips of my handlebars,
a pick-up passing now and then,
the farmer inside raising the index finger
of his left hand precisely
one inch above the wheel, a man
greeting me as a man
for the first time,

the little engine whirring under me,
the scissortails watching from barbed wire,
the road unspooling for thirty miles,
just as my map had promised,
and for the first time I paused
to rest on a long journey,

in this case the town of Corn,
its sole street signal
flashing amber at the crossroads
as I sat at a picnic bench
under the green dinosaur of the Sinclair station,
staring at the town and the little bike
that took me there, feeling,
for the first time, like a traveler,
a sojourner of the plains.

And I drove on to Bessie, where
for the first time I ordered lunch,
reading from the menu in a little café,
speaking seriously and in what I took
to be a manly way, the way of a sojourner,
to the pretty waitress, and what I'd give

today to see myself sitting there in terror
amid the half-dozen farmers eating their chicken-
fried steak, their untanned foreheads white as halos
above their sunburned faces, and
for the first time I left a tip,
counting out the silver gift for her,
and walked out to the bike
that waited for me among pick-ups and tractors,
moving on, for the first time leaving
a woman behind, someone to watch
and acknowledge how the road pulled me away,
someone to keep on looking down that road

long after I'd disappeared, someone who might,
from time to time, look toward the window

and brush the hair from her cheek,
hearing an engine coming from the distance
that swallowed me, for the first time,
that day long ago, a day which for some reason
I am remembering as I sit sipping coffee
in the roadside café, just another rest stop
on the way to Cordell.

OKLAHOMA DUST STORM

~ Carl Sennhenn

A high school speech tournament
took me for the first time to northwestern
Oklahoma after I had been removed
only a short year from Severn and Chesapeake
and Atlantic shores and gently rolling green
mountains of Maryland. Walking across a campus
near where Colorado flattens to become simple
and with no warning at all, strong winds rose,
skies turned a shade I had never known they could
—the color of fury. Then coming at me
from every direction, angry too, strange balls
seemed to take accurate aim at me. Skies and even
larger balls meant only harm. Knowing the Apocalypse
had arrived, I ducked my head, scrambled for safety
despairing all the while that attempts to escape
the end had been forewarned futile
  Watching within a doorway, an Oklahoma native
admired the scene, laughed: "Those sure are big
today, those tumbleweeds" and I, who had known
them only as "tumblin' tumblin' tumbleweeds"
and been urged to "see them tumblin' along"
by Sons of the Pioneers who sang in westerns
in my early seaboard-childhood, laughed too
What do singing cowboys know

Meridian, Oklahoma

~ Joey Brown

Three boys wake up in a town that's not really
a town, weighted down by the early morning
summer, and breathe sour sulphur from the refinery
that clanks and churns or whatever refineries do
to make someone some little bit of money.
It's not them, not their house, so what do they care
but for the nagging smell.

Three boys pump their bicycles on the highway
past the yard of rusted-up drill bits. You'd be afraid
for them were this a highway anywhere else. In the
convenience store they take two Cokes and an
orange Fanta from the lay-down cooler. They like the
pop & sigh the bottle opener makes. When the door
opens again, the air conditioner pleads.

Three boys wait in the parking lot but don't know
they're waiting. Sit astride the bikes, bottles clinking
here and there, don't speak. They stare at the white
day reflecting off the school across the road,
blistering their eyes. You just know they don't
imagine the size of it all. They can't. One of them
keeps firecrackers leftover in his pocket.

A Texan's Fugitive Thoughts

~ Alan Berecka

Heading south just beyond Ada the sign
reads: *Toll $0.65*. I have fed a buck fifty
in change into the plastic Chickasaw
basket on the automated troll that guards
the two-lane turnpike that begins and ends
in the middle of nowhere. I'm thinking,
Com'on run the damn red light, but I once

almost killed a man in this state, a poet
from Chicago who had just brought a cup
of scalding Braum's coffee to his lips as I let go
some dumb-assed quip. He tried not to laugh,
tried not to spit, so he sucked the molten joe
down the wrong pipe. I watched his eyes turn
bloodshot with fear, his thin lips turn blue.
I pounded his bird-like back as his White Sox
cap tumbled. I panicked until he caught a breath.

No, I don't need any trouble here, so I scrounge
under the passenger seat and remember a story
Sam Baker told about a young waitress in Okemah
who when asked if they served sparkling water,
replied, *I suppose, if the light is right*. My finger
hits a nickel under a stale chip. I straighten and toss
the coin into the machine. The light turns green,
and I think, *Next time north, I'll try the casinos*.

41

WIND ON THE LAWTON PLAINS

~ James Ragan

I could watch for days the littering wind gives in to,
as in a train, always to sit alone facing the field
or the boortree as it slaps the sleet toward you
on the lamp-lit pane, and with what skill
to leave the distance passing like a gandy
dancing out of view, while a burdock, taller in its tow
quibbles past, the eyes a mirror withstanding
all that rain can do. It's not as though
the swift train passing leaves you standing still,
nor is it likely the coot that snows in feathers
will out-wing the smoke's long rail.
As long as I am moving forward, I would rather
see the field renewed, a squint of future
    bursting through,
a scud of sunlight, racing through the drumming
    drift of snow.

THE LAND

~ N. Scott Momaday

The first people to enter upon it
Must have given it a name, wind-borne
   and elemental,
Like summer rain.
The name must have given spirit to the land,
For so it is with names.
Before the first people there must have been
The profound isolation of night and day,
The blazing shield of the sun,
The darkness winnowed from the stars –
The holy havoc of myth and origin,
True and prophetic, and inexorable,
Like summer rain.

What was to become of the land?
What was the land to become?
What was there in the land to define
The falling of the rain and the turning of the seasons,
The far and forever silence of the universe?

A voice, a name,
Words echoing the whir of wings
Swelled among the clouds
And sounded on the red earth in the wake
   of creation.
A voice. A name.
Oklahoma.

EL RENO

~ Tony Mares

it was an El Reno motel
down-at-the-mouth and as forlorn
as the crumpled piece of paper
stuck on the dry juniper branch
and fluttering in the wind
in front of the office

my dad parked the 1940 Plymouth
mama and I walked into room #6
outside a discarded baby bassinette
rotted in the blowing dust
whistling east along route 66

now I drive Interstate 40
breeze through El Reno
on my way to Norman
even the ghost of that motel
hard to recall now
but the whiff of the Great Depression
still hangs there in the wind

THE STATE LINE

~ Francine Ringold

A slim line separates the white
from the black, jiggles and twists,
totters like a man
trying to separate the land he once loved
from the clouds he now craves.
They change as the sun bursts through,
sending out the scent of lilacs,
alluring as rest and sleep and soundless
words he can read as he wishes.

What can be done with this horizontal
promise, the wobbling gait, unsteady rune
of time? As the line swings in the wind,
will this state, like a seasoned acrobat,
allow the lift, the detection,
of a new death-defying balance?
Or will it stumble and shake until it folds,
brushed aside by each wind?

How we all yearn to remain steady
on this great walk, yet always —
from the distance — an orange light
beams, then pulses like the fontanel
of each unsuspecting head
growing together like this land
we ache to claim as our own.

OKLAHOMA

(After Langston Hughes)

~ Gary Hawkins

Wind, indifference,
I am held in your trance.

I see the mountain:
Open in the distance.

I see the mountain
With its glassy top.

Indifferent wind,
Lift me up.

PONCA

~ John Yozzo

The Arkansas and its dredge piles
are not easily forgotten haunts.

Hours after the scoops were tethered
we hauled blankets and ice chests
to riverside symposia. Fortified
by Coors, emboldened by nightfall,
we would skinny dip the brown waters.
I stole a glimpse of a girl too forward,
thinking to plant herself too small.

Where Standing Bear a century ago
stood to muse "I gotta get outta this place,"
I was planted, and tonight I can appreciate
the limits of this sheltered prairie town—
the rural air unlike the cities' casserole,
the orange and blue flares and the benzene
tang of our refineries assure skies yet clear.

WORLD'S TALLEST HILL

~ Lauren Zuniga

In Poteau, Oklahoma there stands the world's
tallest hill, one foot shy of being a mountain.
1,999 feet of boasting pride
all the way to the top.
At the top of the hill, shiny trucks
line up like churches.
Giddy swarms of sixteen year old mothers
out late on a Friday night.
Frosted lips and too much eyeliner.
Boys in sagging shorts and big cowboy buckles.
Ice chests full of six-point beer purchased just over
the state line. There is a chrome and bass boxing
match. Tinted windows shaking like bedposts.
Turn it up y'all, this is my jam.
This is weekend medicine.
Billy just got his ink done. It grips tight to his bicep
like Carla, who can't stand the way
Brandy be lookin' at him.
Shit's about to get rowdy tonight.
Right now, you can look out over the hill
and see the 24-hour Wal-Mart glowing
like the queen bee in the hive.
A steady stream of headlights loop around
from Wal-Mart to the movie theatre and back again.
This is how we learn how to move in circles.
How to move in packs.
You can look out over that hill and see Liz.
Tough smirk of a girl. Playing basketball
in the First Baptist parking lot.
Her palms pound so hard they are as calloused
as a dude's. She likes to be called Dude.

Dude will show up at Prom in a tux and leave
with cheeks bloody as corsage.
This is how we learn how to break each other down.
Over at the drive thru, Daniel is working
the closing shift. Saving up
to get the hell out of here.
Hair perfectly spiked over his visor. Uniform collar
popped. No one comments on his mascara
or the touch of concealer.
He is flawless. Brutal wink of a boy.
He's been called fag so much he dropped
a beat behind it and made it his ring tone.
This is how we learn how to man-up.
Rachel works on cars with her dad in the garage.
Glenn Beck rattles through the speakers
like engine grease.
Rachel has been in love with a girl for two years
but she believes in family values. She knows
with all her heart she is going to hell
if she doesn't straighten up.
This is how we get control, fit in.
How we stay small town
in a scary world.
Mr. Elgin shoots BB guns at black boys
for getting white girls pregnant.
Michael climbed to the top of a cell phone tower
to get some attention.
Beth eats Xanax by the fistful.
Jamie built a meth-lab in her sparkly bedroom.
Jenny herds cattle by day, strips at night.
This is how we learn how to cope.
This is how we build pride
one foot shy of a mountain.

ODDS & ENDS

I'll keep us out of war with Oklahoma!

~ KINKY FRIEDMAN
(campaigning for Governor of Texas)

GREENWICH VILLAGE

~ Jim Chastain

It might sound funny
but I'm pretty sure
I've been here before.

Perhaps a speck of dust
that's now some part of me
once blew over Bleeker Street.

Or maybe some cells
from a struggling artist
flaked off

and were carried my way
from Bedford street
by a Northern wind.

Perhaps a teardrop
from some penniless poet
fell to the floor

then evaporated,
forming a sad cloud
that traveled the world

before raining down
on a little farm
in Oklahoma.

THE FAMOUS POETS LIVE IN LOVELY PLACES

~ Carol Hamilton

I read their images, their metaphors.
They must make more money than I do.
They feel the gnaw of beavers
in their forests, all Arcadian,
hear seals' fierce cries in the bay
hanging like a love cry's echo
rippling off through waves of unseen air,
smell the ripe berries clogged
with sweetness in autumn.
I must write of squash bugs,
furry okra, mosquitoes, and the scorching
winds of midsummer.
Some say art is born of hardship…
but I wouldn't bet my cowboy boots on it!

ANOTHER THING TO LAMENT

~ Jerry Bradley

we come to familiar spots to remember
where apprentice angels once gathered
like mosquitoes after a rain
believing the water would never stop

an old house, its slats like hachures
mark some kind of spot
where we could daily dream
the reappearance of ourselves

or see God as something more
than an Oklahoma senator
a perpetual underachiever
who wants us to change

but has run short of commandments
unlike time whose soft petitions
like the water of this deluge
never stanched any flood

New Law Makes Local Poet Nervous

~ Jane Vincent Taylor

Others have book fests, opera and garden expos.
We have gun shows. Ammo. Freedom
and now more freedom: open carry.
Like an old decoy I sit in my local coffee shop.
Post-holiday parents, toddlers in tow, order
the special — peppermint pancakes, dollar-size.
Megan fills the ketchup bottles.
Poinsettias wrinkle and curl. The radio plays Reba.
In walks a vested cowboy sporting a leather holster.
I react the way a gun insists: with fear.
But nearer now,
I see his fancy shoulder bag
holds only oxygen,
precious sips of life — protection,
safety — openly carried, so we can all
breathe a little easier.

Oklahoma

~ Landon Godfrey

Orange trumpet vine plaits through scrub
oak and a chrome-green hummingbird
labors at each fount, the two-way seduction rare
it seems to me.

Red salamanders scrabbling
over red clay. Turtles sunning on helmet-bevel
rocks along the lake shore. Jackrabbit
fur a dopplegänger of dust.

I hate this beauty.
I hate seeing the stars at night,
hearing cricket symphonies
and owls hunting mice.
And vague but vaunted qualities like freedom &
privacy
born of open space
rather than resistance.
The enormous sky widening
into universe, and place singing
the song of place all day, all night.

The only night I've liked here?
When we were walking the dogs late in the evening
and a couple of blocks ahead
we saw a man juggling fire
and when we got to that place
he was gone.
That's the dream—
combustion followed by absence.

WORKSHOPPING ON MT. SCOTT

~ James Hoggard

1

No need, I told them, to look down at their feet.
The wind's too high and the air's too cold for snakes,
but think about what you'd do if one were here –

or a cougar, say, or bison or bear, and for a time,
a longhorn herd grazing near steep rock faces,
and ancient ghosts were finally leaving this place,

like the natives who'd come to take in clean air,
but soon left, then an old wind-singer released
his voice in telling us all the way to sacred space

and its tall grasses. I wanted to draw the students'
attention away from wintering snakes, but cold
as it was, there were airs we had to play in voices

that weren't our own. I gave them fictions to sing,
and giving them those, I gave myself stories, too.

2

So far today, I said, no one has yet taken us to
those turns in our paths where deep images lie,
for all that we've been doing is gazing at blurs

of far away things: everything cold, and the dream
then seized me and put me back on my bike again
on a warmer day, with no icy mist to gut on through,

but my own dream drifting, I couldn't stop shivering,
but others did: they had seen nothing slithering
and they had not tried to ride up Mount Scott.

I had to stop, I had to walk, for I was now in a bad gear
on a shin-splinting downhill run, sleet hard, road slick,
but still so easy to slip off this road and down onto rock,

under sharp wedges of rock where rattlers doze,
where warmth awakes them, but they're slow to appear.

3

This year, though, I'd ridden farther than I had before,
but the grade still steep, I had to get off, had to walk,
had to take another path, but I'd be back to ride again,

to try the hard climb again, and to gauge my pace
on the steep ride down at a speed I could handle:
but chills inside me, I had no way to stop shivering.

So I tried the hard climb again, and on the run down
I held my pace. I'd been careful to hold my pace
at a speed I could handle, but cold in my bones

I found myself not on my bike but by a concrete
table and bench, on a trip now from a different time:
back when I'd been sitting and talking with friends,

all of us gathering voices so different from our own,
all ready now for the fast downhill turns and thrills.

Dog Days

~ Kelli Simpson

I spend hours
roaming the stubbled hayfields,
catching grasshoppers,
and feeding them to the cats.
I've been told that eating too many
will burn them up inside,
but I don't believe it.
The cats don't seem to believe it, either.

It's so hot you can hear it.

There's always a cool spot
in the mud at the edge of the pond,
but you have to crawl under
the willow tree to get there.
I go in slow and watch for water moccasins
curled in the branches above.

I've faced more fearsome monsters.

Sunset spreads like a bruise
across the sky.
The tin roof of the barn,
still warm to the touch,
bears my weight and holds my secrets.
I'm the highest point in the emptiness.

And, the stillness is so vast that I don't make a ripple.

THE OPEN CONTAINER

~ Jim Spurr

Before he died in 1953 at age 39,
Dylan Thomas left a beer can on the podium
at Oklahoma University on his last U.S.A. tour.

Anyhow that's the story I was told as we sat by
a wood burning stove down the road a piece
from a small honkytonk near Pink, Oklahoma.
Just two of us. She was there. Had witnessed it all.
She said.

Here's her story: Thomas was drunk
and everyone put up with it because
he was a great poet and known genius.
The beer brand was Falstaff, she said.
Popular brand at the time. Named, we assume,
after the pleasure seeking Shakespearean
only a mother or drunkard could love.
It had church key openings, which preceded the
aluminum vinyl age of timesaving flip top devices.
The drama department enshrined it. Then later,
when a new theatre was built, it got stolen.
Anyway it was gone.

I believed her, and here's my story:
I'd like to own that can or an exact duplicate.
Then lie about it so I could stand up in some isolated
bar in Anywhere, U.S.A. and quote, "Wild men who
caught and sang the sun in flight... (then some other
line I forgot) do not go gentle into that good night."

PRAIRIE DANCERS: A REVERIE

After Carol Whitney's "Loyal Creek"

~ Carol Davis Koss

Tall grass purls —

    a tuning fork

        sounding desire

An August plain steams —

    red clay churns itself brown

        beneath skin shod soles

    wingèd as tall grass

        tuning desire

REASONS TO STAY INSIDE

~ An-Li Bogan

The grain of fine wind
on the belly of leaf paper
reminds me of a boy I knew
who was shy and careful and
zipped his fly
like it was an art form

today I see him
bubbling up out of the red mud
like a bleeding genesis in swim trunks
I expect a glassy shatter
but the skin of the water
stretches hurriedly
before he buoys through with a rubbery
       Boy-yoy-yoy-yoy-yoing

The crack of Robin's egg is crisp
(as a china doll cutting her fingernails)
the slap of yolk on rock
is full and supple (like satin holding water)
Sage:
the minty mew
the sueded frost
the silver earlobes;
(like scabs of candied peel falling
from the grate of teeth on asphalt)
I wish green would respect its own silence
(seeing as I
am trying so hard to)

BUFFALO GRASS

~ George Wallace

the world is not flat
this is not a poem
and the wind that races
across the rolling hills
of eastern oklahoma
is not the same wind
that used to play its song
on the washboard of injustice
or in the dry gulch of shame
if i could be free with my words
the way that songbirds are free
in april after a tornado has run itself
past town and shook up all the neighbors
i would wrap them up in a thundercloud
i would wrap them up in a rolling rock
i would wrap them up in the red red dirt
that goes this way and that
i would wrap them up in the yellow bark
of a willow tree that i saw growing
on the banks of the north canadian river
if my tongue was more easy
if my mind was more free
if this house was still standing
if my eye was not made so blind
by the way things actually are
in this sad old country sometimes
i would wrap this poem
in oklahoma surplus
i would wrap this poem
in oklahoma mystery
i would wrap this poem

in sunlight and ceiling flowers
and skyscrapers and mermaid memory
and i would roll it on down the road
to a place beyond shawnee
where the world is not flat
and buffalo grass
still grows on a biscuit.

ABUNDANCE

~ Larry Bierman

Big barns so stuffed with rolls of hay
they've busted zippers, popped buttons
bulged corrugated tin.
Cows, big, brown and black, graze pasture
for days and dream of being surrounded
by potatoes and gravy.

The poet gets pissed off that "shoes"
doesn't rhyme with "toes" or "does"
or does it? She
shaves her pits and worries about
what a stumbling block the statement
"nothing is" is.

We love living in front of movie screens,
darkness and the smell of popcorn, teenagers
and Saturday night.
Hollywood is every place—to paraphrase
the laureate Zagajewski, only he meant his
home in Poland.

IF YOU AIN'T GOT THE DO RE MI

~ Jeff Simpson

Someone in the hall yells *Dominoes!*
and just like that I'm shuffling bones
over a card table—the clink-clink sound
like dropping marbles into a wine glass.
Fresh coffee, a slice of pie, and all appears
as worn and smooth as an old Zippo.
We have a radio and a space to eat,
a space to talk, and when you don't
feel like speaking, a space for silence
and an ashtray or a game to pass the time.
I play the double six, sip my coffee,
and gaze into the faces of men who never
went to war, never fought for peace and love
or made it to college, but left the schoolyard
in the seventh grade and spent the last hours
of daylight welding horse trailers from the bare
bones of steel beams, oiled and smoothed,
then transformed into cages to haul
thoroughbreds to Shreveport, Santa Fe,
Oklahoma City, where four hooves
and a beating heart are the means
to a capital gain, a ticket for the small
things in life—new linoleum, new washer
and dryer, new teeth, the new smell
of a new car.
If I'm lucky, I'll lead this hand
with a dime or a nickel—anything
for a break, a good start. I take a bite
of pie. I run my thumb across the pips
on the tile as if reading the future in Braille,
picturing casinos off the interstate

shining like Vegas, Mecca of blinking
lights and three dollar steaks, where before
there were only hay barns and unbroken
lengths of sky. I picture sparrows on a fence,
mockingbirds in the trees, farmers
planting subsidized corn in the dark
knowing it will fail, knowing if the roots
take hold they can fertilize every acre
until it burns and withers back into dust
for the coming spring—anything for a little
disaster relief, a handout in the heartland
because you can forget your stock portfolio,
forget about strapping what's left of your
belongings to a Model T and heading west.
There's no more California, no prospects
of fortune. This state's rush was in '68
when impulsive welders went north to work
the pipeline, sealing gaps with exquisite beads,
pretty as Victorian penmanship.
After all, this is where the wind
comes sweeping down the plains,
where license plates tell us everything is *OK*,
and it is, I suppose, so long as there's honey
in my honey bear and milk in the fridge.
For every grey sky, the kiss of spring.
For every dead field, rodeos in July—
the odor of cotton candy and horseshit,
popcorn and keg beer. We sit in the stands
waiting for a renegade bull or a clown
to get what's been coming for him
his whole life. Strange how much we love
disaster, how I'll watch the Daytona
500 hoping for a collision, praying for a spill,

until it's not so much a race as an assembly
of motorized billboards smashing into one
another at 188 miles per hour—100 more
than the 88 required to get back to the future
and away from clock towers and the pressure
to ensure your own existence.
Someone changes the station and America
sings out on the radio—Crystal Gale followed
by Marty Robins followed by Woody Guthrie
and his tiresome locomotive blues—
song of the dust bowl, song of the banjo,
song of the boxcar and red clay dirt.
I check my watch. I drop a tile and look
for a pattern, though I've got nothing
but a double blank. I think I'm just better
on paper. There's more danger in a Popsicle
stick than my fingertips. The trick is to be
on the go, the way alcoholics' mouths
move even when they're not speaking.
On the muted TV they're showing images
of the Murrah building—song of the Ryder
truck, song of ammonium nitrate.
The hours pile up like seeds in a grain elevator,
but if you got the money, honey, I got the time.
We start another round, draw another hand,
and I wonder about the places
I could've been tonight—song of Astroturf,
song of the reservation, song of the doublewide,
the La-Z-Boy, the microwavable pancake
dinner. The tiles start to resemble a jagged
spine misshapen after years of bad posture.
I try not to overthink the next play.
I tell myself that in the end every move's

the same, so you might as well take off
your coat and drop another quarter, say another
prayer, score the odds on horses and weather,
the likelihood of an early spring—
song of the cattle prod, the seed catalogue,
the convergence of pressure systems
that'll huff and puff and blow your house in.

OKLAHOMA LITANY

~ Wilma Elizabeth McDaniel

Top drawers of memory
never contain anything
of value for me
When wounded
and needing a balm
    I pull out the bottom
drawer
of my mind
marked Oklahoma
which holds a list
of small raw towns
with names of touching beauty
    I recite with touching reverence
    Bowlegs
    Depew
    Pretty Water
    Idabel
        Lone Star
        Gypsy Corner
    Broken Arrow
    Cloud Chief
        until the words
        form a prayer
which I do not understand
    but close the drawer
    with my own Amen

AUTHOR BIOS
and Publication Credits

DOROTHY ALEXANDER is a poet and co-owner of a two-woman independent press that highlights the work of Oklahoma poets. She received the *2013 Carlile Award for Distinguished Service to the Oklahoma Literary Community*, awarded by the Oklahoma Center for the Book and Oklahoma Friends of the Library. "Red Moon Powwow" first appeared in *Cooweescoowee Journal of Art & Letters*, and subsequently in *Lessons From an Oklahoma Girlhood*, Village Books Press (2008).

ALAN BERECKA lives in South Texas. Although a transplanted Texan, he has regularly attended the Scissortail Festival in Ada and has read in Shawnee and Okemah. His book *Remembering the Body* (2011) was published by Oklahoma's Mongrel Empire Press. His latest collection *With Our Baggage* is forthcoming from Lamar University Press.

LARRY BIERMAN—born a third-generation Oklahoman in 1945—grew up in Oklahoma City, studied at Oklahoma City University and graduated from the University of Oklahoma. A writer since Taft Junior High, Larry worked as Poet-in-the-Schools, is a founding member of the Individual Artists of Oklahoma, and is author of four poetry collections. He lives in Norman, Oklahoma.

GEORGE BILGERE'S most recent book of poems is *The White Museum*, chosen by Alicia Ostriker for the 2010 Autumn House Poetry Series. His poems are heard frequently on Garrison Keillor's *The Writer's Almanac*, and he was recently a featured guest on *A Prairie Home Companion*. He teaches at John Carroll University in Cleveland, Ohio. He has a new collection of poems, *Imperial*, forthcoming from the University of Pittsburgh Press. "Cordell" first appeared in *Field*, and then in *The Good Kiss*, University of Akron Press (2002).

AN-LI BOGAN is a senior drama major at Classen School for Advanced Studies in Oklahoma City. She has attended the Oklahoma Summer Arts Institute for Creative Writing for two years and has been published in online magazines and journals. She has spent the last few months writing college essays. They are not as fun as poetry.

JERRY BRADLEY is Professor of English at Lamar University. He is the author of five books including *The Importance of Elsewhere* and *Simple Versions of Disaster*. His poetry has appeared in *New England Review*, *Modern Poetry Studies*, *Poetry Magazine*, and *Southern Humanities Review*. He is poetry editor of *Concho River Review*.

JOEY BROWN is a poet, fiction writer, essayist, and Professor of English at Missouri Southern State University who grew up in Comanche, Oklahoma. Her work has appeared in several literary journals nationwide. A collection of her poems titled *Oklahomaography* was published by Mongrel Empire Press in 2010. "Meridian, Oklahoma" was previously published in *The Chaffin Journal* and was included in the collection *Oklahomaography*.

JEANETTA CALHOUN MISH is a poet whose 2009 collection *Work Is Love Made Visible* was awarded the Oklahoma Book Award, the Western Heritage "Wrangler" award and the WILLA from Women Writing the West. She is the Director of The Red Earth MFA at Oklahoma City University. "The Etymology of Honky Tonk" was previously published in *Work Is Love Made Visible* (West End Press, 2009).

LAUREN CAMP is the author of two volumes of poetry, most recently *The Dailiness*, selected by *World Literature Today* as an "Editor's Pick." A radio producer on Santa Fe Public Radio, Lauren is also a visual artist. Her grandmother was born in and lived her entire 94 years in Oklahoma. www.laurencamp.com. "My Grandfather and

His Eggs" is included in Lauren Camp's collection, *The Dailiness* (Edwin E. Smith Publishing, 2013).

JIM CHASTAIN was a poet, film critic, and attorney for the Oklahoma Court of Criminal Appeals. His memoir, *I Survived Cancer, but Never Won the Tour de France*, made the Top Ten Nonfiction of 2006 by the Austin Chronicle. He published three books of poetry, one of which, *Antidotes and Home Remedies*, was a finalist for the Oklahoma Book Award in 2009. Jim was a good man, a champion of poetry in Oklahoma, and fought cancer for nine years, until he lost on Christmas Eve in 2009. "Greenwich Village" first appeared in his posthumous collection, *Last Supper* (Village Books Press, 2012).

STEPHEN DUNN is the author of sixteen books, including *Different Hours*, which won the 2001 Pulitzer Prize for poetry. Since 1974 he has taught at Richard Stockton College of New Jersey, where he is Distinguished Professor of Creative Writing. "Oklahoma City", from *Different Hours* by Stephen Dunn. Copyright © 2000 by Stephen Dunn. Used by permission of W. W. Norton & Company, Inc.

GEORGE ECONOMOU is the author of thirteen books of poetry and translations, the latest of which are *Complete Plus—The Poems of C. P. Cavafy in English* (Shearsman Books, 2013) and *Ananios of Kleitor* (Shearsman Books, 2009), and he has been named twice as an NEA Fellow in Poetry. He was department chair of English from 1983 to 1990 and Director of Creative Writing from 1991 to 2000 at the University of Oklahoma. "An Evening in Kingfisher" was previously published in: *harmonies & fits*, Point Riders Press, 1987; *Century Dead Center*, Left hand Books, 1997; and *Pomegranate Seeds, An Anthology of Greek-American Poetry*, ed. Dean Kostos, Somerset Hall Press, 2008.

DIANE GLANCY is a professor at Azusa Pacific University. She lived in Oklahoma 1964-1988, traveling for the State Arts Council from which much of her work has come. In 2010 she made a film in Oklahoma, "The Dome of Heaven." Her publications are on her websites, www.dianeglancy.com and www.dianeglancy.org. "Vici, Oklahoma" first appeared in *Iron Woman*, winner of the 1988 Capricorn Prize (New Rivers Press, 1990).

LANDON GODFREY'S first book, *Second-Skin Rhinestone-Spangled Nude Soufflé Chiffon Gown* (Cider Press Review, 2011), was selected by David St. John for the Cider Press Review Book Award. She is also the author of two limited-edition letterpress chapbooks, *In the Stone* (RAPG-funded artist's book, 2013) and *Spaceship* (Somnambulist Tango Press, 2014). "Oklahoma" appeared in *Second-Skin Rhinestone-Spangled Nude Soufflé Chiffon Gown*. Used by permission of the author. www.landongodfrey.com

KEN HADA'S recent poetry collections include Western Heritage Award recipient *Spare Parts*, *The River White: A Confluence of Brush & Quill*, and a cd, *Like Father, Like Son: A Narrative in Poetry & Guitar*. He contributes regularly to *All Roads Will Lead You Home* – a poetry blog available at http://vacpoetry.org/three/. "Yellow Cottonwoods" first appeared in *adaHub*. Vol. 1 issue 5, November 2010, 17.

CAROL HAMILTON is a former Poet Laureate of Oklahoma and has been nominated for a Pushcart Prize five times. She has won a Southwest Book Award, an Oklahoma Book Award, Cherubim Award, Chiron Review Chapbook Award, David Ray Poetry Prize, the Byline Literary Awards for both short story and poetry, and the Warren Keith Poetry Prize. She is a former elementary school teacher, community college and university professor.

JOY HARJO'S seven books of poetry include *How We Became Human- New and Selected Poems*. Her memoir *Crazy Brave*, recently won the PEN USA Literary Award for Creative Non-Fiction. She is working on a musical that will include southeastern indigenous people in the origin story of blues and jazz. She lives in the Mvskoke Nation in Oklahoma. "The Last Song". Copyright © 1975 by Joy Harjo, from *How We Became Human: New and Selected Poems: 1975-2001* by Joy Harjo. Used by permission of W. W. Norton & Company, Inc.

GARY HAWKINS writes poems and writes on poetry; he teaches writing and publishes on pedagogy. His work has appeared in *Virginia Quarterly Review*, *Emily Dickinson Journal*, and other places. A member of the faculty of the writing program, he also serves as associate dean at Warren Wilson College. He lives with his wife, the poet Landon Godfrey, in Black Mountain, North Carolina, one of poetry's most enviable addresses.

JAMES HOGGARD is the author of more than twenty books, including novels, poems, personal essays, short stories, and literary translations. Winner of numerous awards, his work has appeared in *Harvard Review*, *Southwest Review*, *Partisan Review*, *Chelsea*, *Manoa*, and many others. He retired from Midwestern State University as the Perkins-Prothro Distinguished Professor of English.

ABIGAIL KEEGAN is a Professor of British and Women's Literature at Oklahoma City University. She has published *Byron's Othered Self and Voice: Contextualizing the Homographic Signature*, a critical study of gender and sexuality in the *Oriental Tales*, and other essays on literature. Keegan is a poet and former editor of *Piecework: a Poetry Magazine for Women*. She has published three collections of poetry: *The Feast of the Assumptions*, *Oklahoma Journey*, and her latest book, *Depending on the Weather*, was a finalist for the 2012 Oklahoma Book Award. "Pictures of Pioneer Women" first appeared in *Depending on the Weather*, Village Books Press.

CAROL DAVIS KOSS—by birth a New Yorker—has lived in Oklahoma City for over 40 years. She has taught English, Creative Writing, and Remedial Reading from middle school through college; and in venues that range from wealthy suburbs to the South Bronx, from churches to prisons. She is the author of *Chapter and Verse* (1997), *Camera Obscura* (2001 Oklahoma Book Award finalist), and *Painted Full of Tongues* (2002). "Prairie Dancers: A Reverie" first appeared in *Sugar Creek Review* (October/2004).

NORBERT KRAPF, former Indiana Poet Laureate and professor emeritus at Long Island University, lives in Indianapolis. As IPL, he championed collaborations and the reunion of poetry and song. His recent collections include *Songs in Sepia and Black and White* and *American Dreams*, and he held a Creative Renewal Fellowship from the Arts Council of Indianapolis to combine poetry and the blues. "A Red Barn for the Joads" first appeared in *Invisible Presence: A Walk through Indiana in Photographs and Poems*, with Darryl Jones (Indiana University Press, 2006).

QURAYSH ALI LANSANA is author of five poetry books, three textbooks, a children's book, and editor of eight anthologies. He is Associate Professor of English/Creative Writing at Chicago State University, where he served as Director of the Gwendolyn Brooks Center for Black Literature and Creative Writing from 2002-2011. *Our Difficult Sunlight: A Guide to Poetry, Literacy & Social Justice in Classroom & Community* (with Georgia A. Popoff) was published in 2011 by Teachers & Writers Collaborative and was a 2012 NAACP Image Award nominee. *mystic turf*, a collection of poems, was released in 2012 by Willow Books.

TONY MARES is an internationally published poet and author. His books include *Astonishing Light: Conversations I Never Had With Patrociño Barela* (UNM Press, 2010), and *Corazón Del Río* (Voices From the American Land Project, April, 2011). The North American Academy of the Spanish Language will publish his Spanish versions of many of the poems.

JULIA MCCONNELL is a poet and a librarian living in Oklahoma City. She is also the secretary of the Oklahoma Library Association. Julia's work has appeared in *Ain't Nobody That Can Sing Like Me: New Oklahoma Writing*, *Blood and Thunder*, and *Elegant Rage: A Tribute to Woody Guthrie*.

WILMA ELIZABETH MCDANIEL was born in Oklahoma in 1918 and attended schools in Lincoln and Creek Counties. In 1936, economic conditions forced her sharecropper family to migrate west during the Great Depression, and she lived the rest of her life in California's Central Valley where she was known as the "Okie poet." Wilma began writing as a young child, but was not published until she reached her mid-50s. Soon her work became known widely, attracting publishers from California to New York. Her poetry, anthologized in American working-class literature, is uniquely placed by time and geography. Place mattered to her and even though she left Oklahoma, she proudly identified as an Okie and continued to write about Oklahoma all her life. In 2008, the Oklahoma State University Library created, under the direction of Karen Neurohr, Assoc. Professor, an oral history project, *Remembering Wilma Elizabeth McDaniel: Poet and Oklahoma Dust Bowl Emigrant*, to record and preserve the stories of people who knew Wilma. One focus of the OSU Library's Special Collections is an emphasis on the lives of Oklahoma women and the Dust Bowl history. "Oklahoma Litany" ©Wilma Elizabeth McDaniel appeared in *A Prince Albert Wind*, Mother Road Publications, 1994. Printed with permission of the literary

JAMES MCMURTRY—son of acclaimed author Larry McMurtry—grew up on a steady diet of Johnny Cash and Roy Acuff records. His first album, *Too Long in the Wasteland* (1989), was produced by John Mellencamp. In 1996, McMurtry received a Grammy nomination for his Longform Music Video of *Where'd You Hide The Body*. 1997's *It Had To Happen* received the American Indie Award for Best Americana Album. And 2005's *Childish Things* spent six weeks at No. 1 on the Americana Music Radio Chart. In September 2006, *Childish Things* and "We Can't Make It Here" won the Americana Music Awards for Album and Song of the Year, respectively. "Choctaw Bingo" (Shorttrip Music, BMI) appears on the albums *Saint Mary of the Woods* (Sugar Hill Records, Inc. 2002) and *Live in Aught-Three* (originally on Compadre Records, Inc. 2004, now licensed to Lightning Rod Records). Used by permission of the author.

N. SCOTT MOMADAY is a member of the Kiowa Tribe of Oklahoma, and a poet, novelist, playwright, artist and storyteller. He holds a doctorate from Stanford University, and has won the Pulitzer Prize, the Italian Premio Literrario "Mondello," a National Medal of Arts, and a Lifetime Achievement Award from the Native Writers' Circle of the Americas, among many other prizes and honors. In 2007, he was designated Oklahoma Centennial Poet Laureate.

BENJAMIN MYERS is a winner of the Oklahoma Book Award and the author of *Lapse Americana* (New York Quarterly Books 2013) and *Elegy for Trains* (Village Books Press 2010). His poems appear in *32 Poems, Poetry Northwest, Nimrod, Tar River, The Iron Horse Literary Review, Borderlands* and many other journals. "Deep Fork" first appeared in *Plainsongs*, and then in *Lapse Americana*.

JAMES NAVÉ is a poet/storyteller, arts entrepreneur, and public speaking coach. He believes that developing your creative potential is the key to living a productive, happy, free, and successful life. He holds an MFA in poetry from Vermont College. More at: www.jamesnave.com

NAOMI SHIHAB NYE received the 2013 NSK Neustadt Prize for Children's Literature at the University of Oklahoma, nominated by Ibtisam Barakat. Her next book will be *The Turtle of Oman*, fall 2014, from Greenwillow. "Flinn, on the Bus" was reprinted with permission of the author from *19 Varieties of Gazelle*, Greenwillow, HarperCollins, 2002.

RON PADGETT'S *How Long* was a 2012 Pulitzer Prize finalist in poetry. His memoirs include *Ted; Joe;* and *Oklahoma Tough: My Father, King of the Tulsa Bootleggers*. Padgett is a Chancellor Emeritus of the Academy of American Poets. His new book is *Collected Poems*. "Driveway" first appeared in *Collected Poems* (Coffee House Press, 2013).

JAMES RAGAN is an award-winning author of eight books of poetry including his two most recent *Too Long a Solitude* and *The World Shouldering I*. A Fulbright Professor, he has read for six heads of state including Mikhail Gorbachev and Vaclav Havel and is translated into twelve languages. His plays have been staged in the U.S., Beijing, Athens, and Moscow. "Wind on the Lawton Plains" first appeared in *Too Long a Solitude* (University of Oklahoma Press, 2009).

FRANCINE RINGOLD, *Nimrod International Journal*'s Senior Advisory Editor and Editor-in-Chief for over 40 years, completed two terms as Oklahoma's Poet Laureate (2003-2005, 2005-2007). Her book of poems, *Still Dancing*, won the Oklahoma Book Award in 2005. Her books include *The Trouble with Voices: Poetry*, another Oklahoma Book

Award winner; *Every Other One*, with Manly Johnson; and *Making Your Own Mark: Writing and Drawing for Senior Citizens*.

STEVEN SCHROEDER grew up on the High Plains in the Texas Panhandle, where he first learned to take nothing seriously. He currently lives and writes in Chicago. His most recent poetry collections are *Turn* and (with David Breeden) *Raging for the Exit*. More at stevenschroeder.org. "Meditations on a Theme of Sam Baker" first appeared in *All Road Will Lead You Home* at: vacpoetry.org/three

CARL SENNHENN, a native of Annapolis, has gratefully called Oklahoma home since 1951. Retired in 2008 after 50 years teaching children, senior adults, and university and college students, Sennhenn was named Oklahoma Poet Laureate in 2001 and was twice awarded the Oklahoma Center for the Book Award in poetry.

DANIEL SIMON is assistant director and editor in chief of *World Literature Today* magazine at the University of Oklahoma, where he also teaches. A poet and translator, he has poems in *Prairie Schooner* and *Poetry International*. He lives in Norman, Oklahoma, with his wife and three daughters.

JEFF SIMPSON was born and raised in southwest Oklahoma. He is the author of *Vertical Hold*, which was a finalist for The National Poetry Series. His poems have appeared in *Forklift, Ohio; Prairie Schooner; Harpur Palate; Poet Lore*, and others. He now lives in Brooklyn, NY, where he works for *Poets & Writers Magazine* and edits *The Fiddleback*, an online arts & literature magazine. "If You Ain't Got the Do Re Mi" first appeared in *Vertical Hold* (Steel Toe Books, 2001).

KELLI SIMPSON is a poet and blogger from Norman, Oklahoma. She is the co-author (with Shay Simmons and Joy Ann Jones) of the poetry collection *Gemini / Scorpio /*

Capricorn. Her work has appeared in *Poet's Market 2013* and *Emerge Literary Journal.* Find more of her poetry at *Another Damn Poetry Blog.* "Dog Days" first appeared in *Gemini/Scorpio/Capricorn* (ALL CAPS PRESS, 2013).

JIM SPURR is an honorably discharged vet with a B.A. from Oklahoma Baptist University and is a retired insurance adjuster. He lives in Shawnee, Oklahoma with wife Aline. He has read often at the Woody Guthrie Festival in Okemah, OK and the Scissortail Creative Writing Festival at ECU in Ada. Two of his books have been finalists for the Oklahoma Book Award. And he is the co-host of the *Third Thursday* reading in Shawnee.

LARRY D. THOMAS, a member of the Texas Institute of Letters and the 2008 Texas Poet Laureate, has published twenty collections of poetry, most recently *Uncle Ernest* (Virtual Artists Collective, Chicago). His *Larry D. Thomas: New and Selected Poems* was short-listed for the National Book Award. Website: www.LarryDThomas.com

JANE VINCENT TAYLOR is a poet, teacher and librarian. She teaches writing at Ghost Ranch in New Mexico. Her latest book, *The Lady Victory*, has been adapted for the stage and directed by Ann Folino White (MSU Theatre Department). Visit her at janevincenttaylor.blogspot.com

RON WALLACE is an Oklahoma Native of Scots-Irish, Choctaw, Cherokee and Osage ancestry and is currently an adjunct professor of English at Southeastern Oklahoma State University in Durant, Oklahoma. He is the author of six volumes of poetry, and has been published in numerous journals and magazines. "Learning to Speak Choctaw" first appeared in *Cowboys and Cantos* (TJMF Publishing, 2012). Used by permission.
GEORGE WALLACE is an adjunct professor at Pace University and writer in residence at the Walt Whitman Birthplace. Co-founder of the poetry component of the

Woody Guthrie Festival in Okemah, he visits Oklahoma regularly. Other recent appearances include the Robert Burns Center, Gordon Parks Museum, Lowell Celebrates Kerouac, and the National Steinbeck Center. "Buffalo Grass" appeared first in the book *Beauty Parlors, Train Yards and Everything in Between* (Spartan Press, 2014).

JOHN M. YOZZO is a native of Ponca City, OK, a graduate of the University of Tulsa, and—after 34 years teaching in Alabama and Oklahoma—a retired professor of English living in Tulsa. Yozzo has written poems since junior high, but in the spirit of his favorite poet Robinson Jeffers has never fretted to gain an audience.

LAUREN ZUNIGA is a nationally touring poet and author of *The Smell of Good Mud* from Write Bloody Publishing. She is a three-time international slam finalist and was the 2012 Activist in Residence for the University of Oklahoma. She lives with her two kids in a house named Clementine.

Cover Artist Bio:

RICK SINNETT is an American folk artist and native Oklahoman who creates exciting and colorful, larger-than-life paintings. His series of murals along America's famous Route 66 is currently in production. These iconographic murals stem from Sinnett's desire to bring people and their communities together, instilling pride through the power of dynamic imagery. See his work, which also includes serigraphy, stencilmaking, letterpress printmaking, glass etching, and sculpture, at www.mothcollection.com

Graphic Designer Bio:

JEN RICKARD BLAIR is a graphic artist and web designer in Norman, OK. She is the digital media editor for *World Literature Today* where she manages websites for the magazine and its associated literary prizes and festivals. Her portfolio can be viewed at www.jenrickard.com

EDITOR BIO:

Nathan Brown is a musician, photographer, and award-winning poet from Norman, Oklahoma. He holds a PhD in Creative and Professional Writing from the University of Oklahoma and teaches there as well. Mostly he travels now, though, performing readings and concerts as well as speaking and leading workshops in high schools, universities, and community organizations on creativity, creative writing, and the need for readers to not give up on poetry.

He's published nine books: *Less Is More, More or Less; Karma Crisis: New and Selected Poems*—finalist for the 2013 Oklahoma Book Award and Paterson Poetry Prize; *Letters to the One-Armed Poet: A Memoir of Friendship, Loss, and Butternut Squash Ravioli; My Sideways Heart; Two Tables Over* —Winner of the 2009 Oklahoma Book Award; *Not Exactly Job*—finalist for the Oklahoma Book Award; *Ashes Over the Southwest; Suffer the Little Voices*—finalist for the Oklahoma Book Award; and *Hobson's Choice.*

His poems have appeared in *World Literature Today, Concho River Review, Blue Rock Review, Red River Review, Sugar Mule, Di-verse-city (anthology of the Austin International Poetry Festival), Blood and Thunder, Wichita Falls Literature and Art Review, "Walt's Corner" of The Long-Islander newspaper, Oklahoma Today Magazine, Windhover...* among other journals and anthologies.

For more information, to order books, or to book a performance, go to: **brownlines.com**